Original title:
Apple Picking and Wishes

Copyright © 2025 Creative Arts Management OÜ
All rights reserved.

Author: Giselle Montgomery
ISBN HARDBACK: 978-1-80586-363-2
ISBN PAPERBACK: 978-1-80586-835-4

The Pulse of the Season

In orchards bright with fruit so round,
We climb the trees, what fun we've found!
A basket here, a basket there,
We giggle loud, without a care.

The branch bent low, we start to sway,
Our dreams of cider come out to play.
One slip, one trip, a comical fall,
Laughter erupts, echoing through all.

We vow to bite the crispiest treat,
But first, let's dance, let's skip a beat.
With every crunch, a squishy sound,
Our silly faces are blissfully crowned.

We toss the peels and start to shout,
"Who knew this fun? Let's dance about!"
The season's pulse, a quirky buzz,
With joyful hearts, we'll remember this.

So here we stand, hands sticky and bright,
In autumn sun, everything feels right.
With laughter as the sweetest prize,
We'll cherish these moments, our joyful skies.

Kisses of the Wind

The breeze giggles through the trees,
A dance of leaves and buzzing bees.
With every pluck, a grin appears,
As laughter blooms, dispelling fears.

A rush of color, bright and bold,
Each bite is worth its weight in gold.
A slip, a trip, then joy we find,
Such antics leave us all entwined.

Dreams from the Orchard

We climb so high to touch the sky,
With silly hats, we aim to fly.
One plump delight, a tasty treat,
But watch your step, or face defeat!

Under branches, giggles ring,
Like silly birds, we laugh and sing.
Each juicy sphere a gift from trees,
To share a wink and stolen breeze.

The Allure of Juicy Secrets

Whispers in the fruit-laden air,
Temptation's call is everywhere.
With every snack, a tale unfolds,
Of juicy gems and joyful souls.

A bite reveals a secret sweet,
Yet sticky hands can't be discreet.
We barter giggles like fine wine,
In this game, we're all divine.

Rustling Leaves and Hopes

As shadows dance on the ground,
We race for treats that abound.
A prankster's trick, a little tease,
With cheeks like apples, we aim to please.

The orchard sings with whispers bright,
Beneath the stars and soft moonlight.
Our smiles glow, our hearts they soar,
For joy awaits behind each door.

Orchard Dreams Unfurled

In the orchard, laughter spills,
We dance beneath the swaying frills.
With sticky hands and silly grins,
We plot our brews, where fun begins.

Squirrels eye us, plotting schemes,
Stealing thoughts from all our dreams.
With each ripe fruit, a giggle flies,
As we chase down the buzzing pies.

Harvesting Hope Beneath the Boughs

Under trees with limbs that sway,
We dream of treats, both sweet and fray.
With baskets full of juicy glee,
The fruit can hardly stay on free.

A wink from branches, oh so sly,
As whispers tickle from the sky.
We gather hopes in every bite,
While worms plan dance-offs in delight.

The Cider's Whispered Secrets

A bubbling brew, that's what we seek,
In the laughter, cider speaks.
It tickles noses, causes cheer,
Each sip a giggle, loud and clear.

We stomp around, like tiny feet,
In every drop, there's something sweet.
Beneath the press, our dreams will flow,
With all those fruits, we steal the show.

Baskets Full of Yearning

With woven baskets, dreams in tow,
We march with gusto, full of glow.
Each treasure found is met with glee,
As we shout out, "Look! That one's me!"

Amidst the harvest, friends galore,
Swapping stories, laughs, and more.
A festival of joy we weave,
In every plea, we do believe.

Serenity Under the Canopy

A basket swings from side to side,
With hopes of fruit, we're filled with pride.
The branches bob, they seem to tease,
As squirrels chatter high in the trees.

We climb a bit, we scoff and jest,
In our quest for the very best.
With each pluck comes a silly cheer,
As we dodge the bees buzzing near.

Oh, the thrill of that juicy bite,
Is it day or is it night?
With sticky juice that dribbles down,
Who cares? We laugh as we spin around.

In this place of dreams so sweet,
We've found a joy that can't be beat.
Underneath the sky so blue,
Handfuls of fun for me and you!

Nature's Silent Promises

Amongst the leaves, our giggles soar,
Shh! Don't scare the fruits we adore.
With stealth and grace, we make our way,
As nature's secrets beg us to stay.

Each plump orb hanging on a thread,
Is a challenge we all have said.
A misstep here, a tumble there,
Laughter erupts into crisp, cool air.

The ground is soft, we sink and slip,
Down we go, into a fitful trip.
Our dreams are tangled in leafy charms,
While nature hums, inviting our arms.

When all's collected, time flies fast,
We reminisce of the fun we've amassed.
With full hearts and baskets wide,
We roam the hills, side by side!

Laughter in the Fields

Fields of green stretch far and near,
With every cackle, life feels clear.
The fruits hang low, just out of reach,
As we attempt our finest speech.

"Don't grab that one!" a friend will shout,
Yet ripe and red, it calls us out.
Our jokes fly higher than the sun,
With each new catch, we've had such fun.

Between the rows, we sneak and dash,
Through golden grains, we make a splash.
The wind will tease, it waves goodbye,
Yet here we grow, our spirits high.

In the end, we're all a mess,
Full of giggles, joy, and jest.
With every scoop, we taste the day,
In this slice of life we play away!

Handpicked Dreams

With gloves on hand and hearts aglow,
In a sea of green, we move to and fro.
Giggling dreams mix with whispers sweet,
Each wishing bite, a special treat.

Around each corner, mischief lurks,
Caught in the act while the sunlight works.
A hefty thud, a fruit rolls down,
Our laughter echoes, no need to frown.

In this orchard of delight and glee,
We dodge the branches, come dance with me.
Surprises hidden in every hue,
As funny tales sprout anew.

With baskets brimming, we take a pause,
Creating memories that get applause.
So here we stand, in joy's embrace,
Chasing sheer fun at our own pace!

Memories Caught in the Breeze

In the orchard, laughter soars,
Bobbing heads like silly boars.
With baskets full, we start to trip,
Stumbling 'round, we let it rip!

A cheeky squirrel steals our snack,
We chase him down, no looking back.
With sticky hands and giggles wide,
We're on a fruity joyride!

Beneath the Crimson Sun

The sun is bright, the sky a show,
We play a game of toss and throw.
A rogue fruit lands upon my head,
   I laugh so hard, I nearly fled!

Under branches, we take our stand,
   Juicy bites slip from our hand.
With every giggle and cheeky grin,
   We make a mess, let fun begin!

A Tapestry of Seasons

Trees wear crowns of red and gold,
In this place, bright tales unfold.
My friend and I, we run in glee,
I swear a branch just winked at me!

We stack our finds, a fruity tower,
Then watch it topple, such sweet power.
With juice-stained shirts and laughs galore,
In this moment, who could ask for more?

Chasing Shadows in the Orchard

We dash between the shadows long,
Singing silly, goofy songs.
An errant fruit takes a daring dive,
Landing near where giggles thrive!

Cider dreams float on the breeze,
As we hunt for hidden keys.
For laughter is the sweetest fruit,
In our chaotic, fun pursuit!

Echoes in the Orchard

In the orchard, I took a swing,
Fell in a heap, oh what a thing!
Baskets toppled, fruit took flight,
A scramble ensued, what a sight!

Squirrels giggled from a high branch,
I yelled, 'Oh come on, give me a chance!'
With every slip, I laughed out loud,
Nature's circus, it made me proud!

A rogue apple hit me right on the head,
I swore I heard the old tree said,
"Next time, try a little more grace!"
But how can you laugh in such a place?

The ground's a mess, but I don't care,
I'll leave my worries hanging in air,
For every fruit that I did miss,
My heart bloomed with a happy bliss!

Sunlit Wishes

Under the sun, I found my groove,
Plucking fruit in a silly move,
I wished for luck with each bright pick,
But tripped on a root; oh, what a trick!

A bird chuckled from a nearby tree,
"Who knew harvesting could be so free?"
With bruised toes, I bounced in delight,
Surrounded by laughter, what a sight!

The juice dribbled down my cheek,
I smirked and said, 'Hey, who needs a sneak?'
My brother laughed, "You're quite the sight!"
"Just wait till dinner, it'll be a fight!"

So I gathered up what I could find,
Throwing wishes and giggles behind,
In this moment, all seemed just right,
Sunlit dreams danced into the night!

A Dance of Gnarled Branches

Gnarled branches twist and sway,
As I leap like a kid in play,
I clutched a branch, what a cluck!
Giggling squirrels mocked my luck!

The apples teetered on their posts,
With every step, I merited boast,
"Look at me, I'm an orchard star!"
Then down I fell, the fanciest jar!

My friends all roared, they rolled with glee,
"Is that the dance? Just wait and see!"
With every tumble, my heart would soar,
Behind my blunders, laughter galore!

As the sun dipped low, we made a pact,
To cherish joy, that's a fact,
With chipped mugs and a feast set wide,
We raised a toast to the humorous ride!

Rustic Reveries

In fields so green, we had our fun,
With laughter ringing, we all would run,
Gathering treasures from trees so stout,
Imagining games with each little spout!

A bravado shout, I climbed with flair,
But slipped right down, oh, the berry flare!
Rolling downhill, it couldn't be less,
A jumbled mess, but I felt so blessed!

We tossed the fruit like silly balls,
With sticky hands, we'd beckon the walls,
To tell our tales of grand escapes,
While dodging grins and playful shapes!

Night rolled in, we toasted our schemes,
As rustic dreams merged with moonlit gleams,
Silly wishes under starry light,
In our heart's orchard, everything's right!

Fruitful Aspirations

In the orchard where laughter grows,
We reach for dreams as high as those!
With our hands outstretched, we take a chance,
Hoping for fruit, not just a glance.

A ladder tilts, oh what a sight!
Someone's hat takes off in flight.
We giggle as we try to catch,
A floating cap with quite the match!

With baskets full and grins so wide,
We may just slip and take a ride.
A tumble here, a flip right there,
And giggles echo through the air.

So here's to joy in all we seek,
Let's grab some snacks and take a peek!
With every bite, our spirits grow,
In this silly, fruity, lively show!

Baskets of Hope

With baskets large, we come prepared,
For treasures found, we are ensnared.
The trees above bear fruits aglow,
Where hopes hang ripe, waiting to show.

We spot a pear; it's round and plump,
I trip and land with quite a thump.
The fruits release a hearty sound,
As giggles spring right from the ground.

The sun shines bright, we proudly cheer,
"Let's gather more, there's joy right here!"
But slips and tricks become the norm,
As laughter dances, chaos is born.

We fill our baskets, oh what fun,
Each fruit a wish: for everyone!
And when the day draws softly near,
We'll make a toast with pear juice beer!

The Juicy Bounty

In fields of sweetness, under sun,
We hunt for treasures, oh what fun!
With every pluck, a giggle peeks,
Some scratches made, but laughter speaks.

A splash of juice upon my face,
Turns this adventure into a race.
With sticky hands and beaming grins,
We find more fruit, the smiles begin.

"Oh look, a fruit the size of me!"
We hoot and holler with pure glee.
A bite so sweet, it makes us dance,
With juice running wild, we take a chance.

And as the sun begins to set,
We fill our baskets, not a fret.
Our spoils are silly, fun, and bright,
In juicy dreams, we end the night!

Secrets Beneath the Trees

Beneath the branches, secrets hide,
In cracking husks, the fun resides.
A rustle here, a whisper there,
As critters munch on fruity fare.

We bend and stretch to see what's there,
A cunning crow gives us a stare.
With flapping wings, it caws out loud,
"Leave some for me!" it sings so proud!

A bit of mischief, a prank or two,
As friends chase shadows, laughter flew.
"Catch that squirrel!" one comically yells,
While slipping down amongst the shells.

So gather 'round, let's share a tale,
Of fruity fights and winds so frail.
With every fruit, a secret found,
In giggles shared beneath the ground!

Sunkissed Moments

In the garden, we play and climb,
With baskets too big, we're running out of time.
A squirrel laughs, steals one fruit,
As we chase him, it's truly a hoot!

The sun is high, our faces bright,
With sticky hands, we're quite a sight.
We tumble and fall, a giggly crew,
Dreaming of pies, and what we'll do!

Fruit on our heads, like crowns we wear,
Competing for the quirkiest affair.
With silly dances, we fill the air,
Each moment shared, a gem so rare.

At day's end, we gather round,
Our bounty vast, a feast renowned.
With each ripe pick, we share a grin,
In this sweet chaos, the joy begins!

Lanterns of Desire

In the twilight glow, we chase delight,
With laughter ringing loud through the night.
A green one's tossed, we all duck low,
The one that laughs last is sure to know!

Twinkling stars above, we make a scene,
As harvest dreams turn bright and green.
We trip and tumble, a merry band,
With fruit in hand, it's simply grand!

The shadows dance, and we join the play,
Making wishes as we fray.
Each wish a joke, a tale we spin,
In this joyful mess, we all win!

As lanterns glow, we toast our quest,
With every bite, we feel so blessed.
In this orchard chaos, we find our tune,
With every glimmer, we laugh at noon!

Ripe with Possibility

With baskets swinging, we march in line,
A fruit-filled adventure, oh so divine!
With giggles loud, and feet so fleet,
We reach for the branches, what a feat!

The branches bow with their shiny charms,
Inviting us in with their fruity arms.
A slip and a slide, we tumble down,
Who knew that grapes would wear a crown?

We craft a crown from cupped hands,
Declaring ourselves, the fruit kings of lands.
Each bite a treasure, sweet surprise,
With every chuckle, our joy will rise!

With every harvest, wishes abound,
In this quirky place where fun is found.
In giggles and bites, we find our peace,
In ripe joy, our spirits increase!

The Elixir of the Grove

In the grove where laughter spills,
We concoct ideas, our minds with thrills.
A twist of fate, with every snack,
We plan our heist for the next big stack!

Each fruit we gather, whispers of cheer,
Boosting our spirits, no room for fear.
With every bite, a new tale blooms,
In goofy antics, mischief looms!

A secret recipe, we mix with glee,
With humor as zest, oh can't you see?
The elixir of joy, we hand it out,
Here's to silliness, of that no doubt!

As dusk arrives, we toast to the day,
With sticky fingers, we shout hooray!
In this grove of dreams, we all unite,
Making memories that feel just right!

A Lullaby of Ripe Red Marvels

In the orchard, giggles soar,
Chasing shadows, hearts explore.
With baskets full of treasures bright,
We laugh until we're lost from sight.

Juicy jewels in hand, we race,
A sticky grin on every face.
The ground is soft, the trees are high,
We'll toss a fruit and kiss the sky.

Tiny critters, watch your step,
As we dive where the sweetness crept.
A fruity war, oh what a blast!
Who knew the fun would go so fast?

When twilight whispers, we'll retreat,
With red-stained cheeks, we find our seat.
Beneath the stars, we'll dream tonight,
Of harvests big and laughter's flight.

Beneath the Canopy of Wishes

Giggles twine with golden rays,
In the trees where critters play.
Whimsies dance on leafy greens,
Where each branch hides silly scenes.

Oh, the splat when fruits collide,
Laughter bursting like the tide.
Running in a giddy chase,
Slipping through the wild embrace.

The sky is bright, a clownish blue,
As dreams like candy, stick like glue.
We'll gather laughter, count our bounces,
Creating moments, laugh-filled ounces.

When shadows stretch, we'll sing a tune,
Beneath the stars, the glowing moon.
In every heart, a silly wish,
To dance with fruits and giggle swish.

The Perfumed Zephyr's Gift

A breeze of sweetness fills the air,
As giggles burst, without a care.
Swinging high, we reach for fun,
With every toss, the day is won.

Branches bow, a gentle sigh,
A fragrant feast drifts by and by.
Do we share or start a fight?
With every splat, it feels so right!

The petals twirl, a funny play,
As pickers stumble on their way.
Who knew this hunt would bring such glee,
With every fruit, a jubilee!

When dusk descends, the laughter lingers,
Sticky thumbs and joyful zingers.
Underneath the fading light,
We gather dreams to take our flight.

Picking Sunlight from Branches

In the orchard, sunbeams glint,
With each pluck, our joys are mint.
Branches bowing, laughter reigns,
With silly games and fruity gains.

A tumble here, a splash of red,
We're rolling back with laughter fed.
Giddy chases, giggles sprout,
With every toss, we twist about.

As shadows lengthen, we rejoice,
In fruity mess, we find our voice.
Sweetened dreams in every bite,
We'll sing until we reach the night.

The stars will wink, our hearts will glow,
In the orchard, joy will flow.
With every laugh, the whispers swirl,
In this sweet, bright, funny world.

The Enchantment of Trees

Beneath the branches, laughter flows,
Where squirrels plot and mischief grows.
With baskets ready, we take our stand,
As apples giggle, oh so grand.

A tug of fruit, a gentle pluck,
The trees conspire, they play their trick.
One slips away with a cheeky toss,
We chase it down—oh, what a loss!

In sunny patches, we dance around,
While sticky fingers race the ground.
A revelry in every bite,
These crunchy jewels are pure delight.

So gather 'round, let's make a scene,
In orchard realms, we reign as queens.
With giggles bursting, souls ablaze,
In tree-clad wonder, we spend our days.

Beneath an Orchard Sky

We roam beneath the leafy sway,
With petulant fruit in bright array.
Each step we take is met with glee,
As apples tumble down like tea.

A leap to snag the highest prize,
But plop! They fall to our surprise.
Laughter bounces, oh what a sight,
As apples juggle, it's pure delight.

The worms are plotting in their lair,
While bees join in—a buzzing affair.
We dodge and dart, a game we play,
In nature's court, it's our fine day.

So swing your arms, and touch the sky,
Let's toast to fruits that never lie.
Under this bough, let's share a grin,
In fruity frolic, we all win!

Pathways Lined with Fruits

On pathways trailed with juicy cheer,
Where fruits parade, it's crystal clear.
With mischief brewing and humor's might,
We navigate this whimsical sight.

A plop here, a thud there,
The orchard road is quite the lair.
With every step, potential knocks,
As apples tumble, out of their socks!

We weave through rows like ribbons spun,
With giggles bubbling, it's all in fun.
Some ripe and ready, some still green,
A delightful feast that's quite obscene.

So let's embrace this fruity spree,
Beneath the sun, wild and free.
With laughter echoing through the trees,
We'll take our share of fruity tease.

Fingers Stained with Nature

With fingers stained in colors bright,
We venture forth to a fruity fight.
The trees are laughing, can't you see?
They toss their treasures down with glee.

A scoop, a toss, a running chase,
We race each other, a silly pace.
Our basket swells with every haul,
As nature's treats begin to sprawl.

The juice runs wild, oh what a mess,
A fruity war? Now that's success!
We gather round, finger-licking good,
In this joyous commune of cheeky food.

So cheers to fun, and fruit-stained days,
In orchards bright, we'll sing and play.
With nature's bounty, we take our stand,
Stained fingers, giggles, life is grand!

A Mosaic of Flavors

Beneath the trees, we dance and sway,
A game of toss with fruit on display.
Laughter erupts, a pit takes flight,
"Just a snack!" we guffaw with delight.

Buckets brim with colors so bright,
Crisp and juicy, what a sight!
An accidental slip, a tumble, a fall,
"Harvesting fun!" we're having a ball!

Sticky fingers, everyone's a chef,
Mismatched pies, but who needs finesse?
Flavor brawl with each crunchy bite,
Who knew the orchard held such height?

So gather round, let's eat and play,
In this sweet mess, we'll always stay.
With giggles twinkling like stars in the dark,
We'll treasure this taste - our laughter, our spark.

The Orchard's Secrets

In the orchard, whispers float on the breeze,
"Did you hear? They got lost in the trees!"
Round the trunks, like squirrels, we navigate,
Tripped on roots, but it's all first rate.

Fruits like globes, some plump, some small,
A debate on which one's the best of all.
A worm peeks out, quite the cheeky chap,
"Just a little taste!" we act like a sap.

Raucous laughter as we brave a bite,
With every crunch, we feel delight.
But watch your step, don't meet that branch,
Leaving us giggling, in a dance-like trance.

So we gather 'round with a basket of dreams,
Facing the day with our giggly schemes.
For under the branches where the apples gleam,
We'll share every silly moment, beam by beam.

Sunlit Reveries

Sunshine dapples through the leaves above,
While we rally round, all laughter and love.
Aim for the highest, a fruity affair,
Missed the mark? Who cares! It's all in the air!

Swing that arm, give it a whirl,
"Catch that juicy!" A fruit-flavored twirl.
But oops, it lands in the neighbor's yard,
"Thanks for the snack!" we holler, not barred.

Tickled by breezes that play with our hair,
Squeezed in this magic, we giggle and stare.
With stitches of joy, we all take a chance,
In this orchard ballet, we twirl and prance.

So here's to the day, with laughter that lingers,
And sticky surprises on curious fingers.
We'll sip on bright sunlit dreams this way,
In merry embrace of our fruitful play.

Savoring the Moment

Amidst the branches, we chuckle and cheer,
Each fruit brings a tale that we hold dear.
A plop, a squirt, and then laughter erupts,
"Sweet disaster!" we shout, as the juice interrupts.

Giggles ring out like chimes in the air,
What's more fun than this fruity affair?
Saucy concoctions dish up the cheer,
Pies made with chaos, oh dear, oh dear!

Fingers sticky, hearts wide and free,
We'll find fun in our folly, that's the key.
Roaming the rows with our baskets in tow,
Creating delicious moments, go with the flow!

So here's to flavors, both silly and bright,
In every big bite, we chase pure delight.
And at the end of this sweet frenzy,
We'll savor the memory—our orchard spree!

Echoes of Sweetness

Up in the trees, I stretch and sway,
Hoping for one that won't roll away.
My basket's too small, oh what a plight,
Ants at my feet join the fruit-finding fight.

The branches they creak, they're testing my might,
I clutch at a branch, it feels just right.
But wait, oh dear, my hat takes flight,
Now it's a party in the sunlight's light!

Climbing back down, slightly out of breath,
I spot a worm's smile, can it be my death?
With every ripe treasure comes a funny twist,
Such is the joy that we can't resist!

So off to the basket, with giggles and glee,
I plop in my finds, one, two, three.
The day wraps us up in a sweet, sticky song,
Who knew a tree could feel so wrong!

Harvested Hopes

In the golden orchard, it's a cause for cheer,
With friends like these, no room for fear.
A ladder wobbles, my heart does race,
But up I go, it's a wild goose chase!

Each fruit I pluck, a wish in disguise,
But what if they're sour, oh what a surprise!
Laughter erupts as I take a bite,
My face scrunches up, a comical sight.

The sun starts to dip, our mission in tow,
I reach for the highest, with an awkward throw.
It's a dance with the branches, a fruit-fueled affair,
While wasps buzz around, like they're part of the flair!

With baskets all full and a grin ear to ear,
We toast with our harvest, let's give a cheer!
For every odd moment, a memory blooms,
In this funny escapade, joy always looms!

The Glow of Golden Days

Ooh, look at that glimmer, it's shining so bright,
Caught in a branch, what a hilarious sight!
I wiggle and giggle, reaching just so,
And somehow end up with a nose full of dough!

With each tiny apple I toss to my mate,
Our aim's getting worse—it's becoming first-rate!
Yet, laughter resounds, a melodic score,
While squirrels throw acorns like they're at war.

The sun starts to fade, painting things gold,
Our baskets are heavy, our stories unfold.
As I trip on a root, what a graceful fall,
"Do you think this counts?" I croak, "as part of it all?"

But side by side, we share the fun,
In this orchard game, we've already won.
For with every laugh piped in crisp afternoon,
Who knew fall's bounty could hum a sweet tune?

Whispers of Fruit

In the orchard's embrace, where laughter takes flight,
I fumble and stumble, with comical might.
The fruits tease and taunt from their leafy perch,
While I trip on a twig, oh what a lurch!

With a hop and a skip, I grab at a peach,
And a tumble reveals all the worms' little speech.
A squishy surprise, it rolls down the slope,
While a rogue crow caws, full of cheek and hope.

As shadows grow long, and the breeze sings a tune,
We dance around baskets, like spoons on a moon.
The jests and the jives, they fill up the air,
While laughter cascades, a jewel we all share.

So here's to the moments that make our hearts glow,
In the orchard of jokes, where the good times flow.
Finding joy in the fruits, even funny mistakes,
Is the secret to life, for goodness' sakes!

The Orchard's Embrace

In fields of red and green so bright,
I climbed a tree quite out of sight.
I snagged a fruit, with sticky hands,
And dreamt of pies in far-off lands.

The branches creaked, they squeaked and swayed,
I thought of what I might get paid.
A basket full or just a few,
I hope the fruit is fresh and new.

A squirrel scolded me for my loot,
He claimed the best, a perfect fruit.
I laughed and said, "You're quite a tease,
Now hand it over, pretty please!"

With juice that drips and laughter raised,
I danced around, completely dazed.
Oh orchard fair, so full of cheer,
I'll come back often, never fear!

Plucking Dreams

A basket waiting, sturdy, strong,
I ventured forth, I won't be long.
With every reach, I swayed and bent,
A branch gave way, it was well-meant.

I plucked a snack that made me grin,
The juiciest prize, a sweet win-win.
But down I tumbled, flopped right flat,
Chasing crumbs off of the mat.

The sun was bright, my hat flew high,
A fruit flew past like it could fly.
"Oh no, that better not be mine!"
I chased my dreams through rows that shine.

Later I sat, my harvest grand,
But found only cider in my hand.
A wish for pies turned to a drink,
Next time I'll take a moment to think!

Nature's Gratitude

Beneath the boughs, a sight to behold,
My heart was light, my spirit bold.
I laughed with trees, they laughed right back,
In every corner, a picnic snacked.

With every bite, a giggle arose,
Each crunch a quick quip that comes and goes.
Who knew that nature brought such fun?
Not only fruit, but joy and sun!

I tossed my worries, they floated away,
As squirrels conspired in a game to play.
Who'd get the snack, who'd grab the prize?
It was a party in nature's guise.

So here's to trees that make us sing,
Where every pluck can branch a fling.
Hold tight your joy, let laughter lift,
For nature's bounty is the best gift!

An Invitation from the Trees

Come one, come all, let's have some fun,
An orchard feast beneath the sun.
Join in the dance, let laughter grow,
With golden fruit all in a row.

A tree invites, with branches wide,
To pluck a snack and take a ride.
I swung from limbs, oh what a sight!
I lost my hat! It took to flight!

The fruits of labor, juicy dreams,
Dripped down my chin, just like the streams.
I made a crown, an artful piece,
But squirrels exclaimed, "Hey, that's our feast!"

So gather near, bring zestful cheer,
For every bite sparks joy, my dear.
With every chuckle, wishes flow,
These trees know how to steal the show!

The Promise of Autumn

In the orchard, laughter rings,
Beneath the trees, joy takes wings.
With baskets wide, we dance around,
As juicy treasures tumble down.

A squirrel yells, 'Hey, that's my stash!'
We giggle, run, and make a dash.
With sticky hands and silly grins,
Who knew such fun would lead to sins?

A harvest moon beams overhead,
We've traded sleep for crumbs and bread.
In this frenzy, we stand so true,
Among the chaos, I pick you!

Then off we go, with bites to share,
A silly fight? There's hardly a care.
For in each crunch, we hear the cheer,
Autumn's promise brings us near.

Lustrous Harvest

A shiny orb upon a tree,
It winks at us, oh what a spree!
With every reach, a giggle bursts,
Our clumsy dance, the sweetest thirst.

We climb and tumble, oh what a sight!
The ground says, 'Stay, you're too bright!'
Yet up we go, with joy untold,
Like kids unleashed, but none too bold.

Each fruit we pluck calls out our name,
Like friendly ghosts in this sweet game.
The taste of mischief fills the air,
As laughter blends with autumn's flair.

We gather round with spoils so grand,
With silly dreams and sticky hands.
In every bite, a chuckle rests,
A harvest rich with silly quests.

From Branch to Heart

Once in a grove of sweet delight,
We aimed our sights with all our might.
A fallen branch, a clever ruse,
Our game of catch? Let's not refuse!

With fruits a-flying, we waddle and squeal,
Who needs a meal when joy's the real deal?
Cider spills as we laugh out loud,
In this frolicsome, goofy crowd.

A rogue wind blows, a cap flies high,
"Not my tresses!" a friend will cry.
Yet in this mess, we thrive and glow,
With every toss, our spirits flow.

So here's to the fun that fills our day,
In scrappy boots, we shout hooray!
For every pluck is filled with heart,
From silly games, we'll never part.

Beneath the Canopy

Beneath the leafy, speckled shade,
We crafted dreams; oh, a parade!
With basket bets and sassy flair,
Who'll snag the biggest? Let's declare!

The branches creak with every step,
As giggles echo, our secret kept.
A fruit flies by, heads whip to see,
So many tosses, wild and free!

Each juicy snack, a prize to munch,
Uneasy strolls and a mighty crunch.
We'll trap the sun with smiles so bright,
In this sunny mess, we feel so right.

So here's to us, with silly glee,
Our harvest dreams, a tangled spree.
With every laugh, the heart takes flight,
Beneath the leaves, we hold on tight.

The Garden's Delight

In the garden, I prance with glee,
A ladder wobbles, oh dear me!
Fruits hang low, a tempting sight,
But my trusty shoes just don't feel right.

Fingers sticky, a cheeky grin,
Caught a slight whiff of sweet, ripe sin.
With every bite, I dance and twirl,
But watch out for that rogue squirrel!

Caught in a battle over a peach,
The squirrel's fast, it's quite a reach!
As I shout in jest, 'It's mine to claim!'
He rolls his eyes, "This isn't a game!"

Baskets overflow, laughter's loud,
With every stumble, I feel so proud.
Who knew fruit could spark such cheer?
Next year, I'll bring a friend or two here!

Nature's Palette

Beneath the trees, colors burst bright,
A fruity canvas, what a sight!
Tangled branches, a playful maze,
I lose my way in the sun's warm rays.

The orange one winks, "Pick me, please!"
While the red one shouts, "I'm a tease!"
Giggling frantically, I trip on a root,
Wobbling now, I'm a fruit-loving brute!

The green ones chuckle, "You look a sight!"
"Just one more laugh, then it's out of sight!"
With baskets bulging, the fun won't stop,
But oh dear me, watch that last hop!

Laughter lingers, a joyous sound,
In nature's arms, I feel unbound.
Through all the mischief and fruity spree,
This garden brings out the kid in me!

Celestial Harvest

Under the stars, I take my stand,
A glowing moon, fruit in hand.
What's that noise? A comet's flight!
Is it jealous of my tasty bite?

Gravity's tricky, I leap and sway,
Harvesting dreams, in my playful way.
An orange drips, a showy splash,
"Watch out for that!" I shout with a dash!

The night's alive with giggles and cheer,
While constellations watch, oh so near.
"Catch me if you can," I tease the breeze,
But the stars just chuckle, "Oh, if you please!"

With each silly slip, the stars weave tales,
Of fruity adventures and comical fails.
Under this sky, my wishes unfurl,
In this cosmic garden, I'm just a whirl!

In Search of the Golden Fruit

With a map in hand, I start my quest,
To find the fruit that's deemed the best.
Golden glowing, it's rare indeed,
But my compass spins, oh what a lead!

Through thorny bushes and giant weeds,
My sneakers squelch on juicy seeds.
A rabbit hops by, with a knowing look,
"Follow your nose, not any book!"

Then the golden glow, it catches my eye,
A treasure! Real fruit, oh my, oh my!
But just as I reach, a cheeky crow flies,
"Sorry, my friend, no pies in the skies!"

With laughter echoing, I take a seat,
The journey's the fun, not just the treat.
Though I might leave with no golden prize,
The joy of this chase keeps my spirits high!

Whispers of Joy in Every Fruit

In orchards ripe, we climb so high,
To reach for treats beneath the sky.
Plump and round, each orb a jest,
With laughter bubbling, we feel blessed.

One slipped and fell, a comical sight,
We giggle as we dodge and fight.
For every crunch, a joke we tell,
In every bite, we taste the spell.

The branches bend with giggles near,
As we concoct a fruit-filled cheer.
With sticky hands, our faces gleam,
Each pick, a wacky, sunny dream.

At dusk we sit, our bounty bright,
Recalling tales in fading light.
The fruits of fun in every shade,
A harvest of joy that won't soon fade.

Sun-Kissed Moments of Gratitude

Under the sun, we gather round,
In giggles, happiness is found.
A basket here, a hat askew,
Together we share this golden view.

Juicy gems, we toss and play,
Who can catch the best today?
Laughter echoes, and time does pause,
Thankful hearts for nature's cause.

With every splash of fruit on clothes,
Comes more laughter, goodness flows.
A sticky treat, a silly dance,
Who knew our day would bring this chance?

As sun dips low, the fun won't cease,
In every bite, we find our peace.
A toast with juice, let's celebrate,
For memories made, we just can't wait!

The Wish Bone of Autumn

In fields so wide, we make our claim,
To gather goodies, it's all a game.
With wishes whispered, we explore,
No magic needed; we just want more!

A quirky dance among the trees,
With playful tricks and silly pleas.
We chase the squirrels, keep them in sight,
While dreaming of treats to fill the night.

A giant fruit, I take a chance,
I trip and fall—oh, what a dance!
In laughter, wishes float on air,
With every bite, we're free from care.

The season's gifts bring joy and cheer,
With every crunch, our hearts draw near.
Let's gather round, a toast, a cheer,
For every wish fulfilled this year!

Reverie in Shades of Scarlet

In orchards bold, the colors call,
With scarlet hues, we have a ball.
We climb and slip, a joyous mess,
With every laugh, we feel the best.

A silly sight, my friend, you know,
Lost in fruit, we steal the show.
Each juicy bite a tale unspun,
In every giggle, we've already won.

A friendly contest, who can eat more?
With fruity faces, we all adore.
Each stab of laughter brightens the day,
As we indulge and play away.

As twilight paints the world anew,
We dance in shadows, hearts so true.
With cheeks aglow, we dream and scheme,
In every moment, we reign supreme!

A Journey in the Orchard

In an orchard so grand, I took a stroll,
Where trees wore colors of sun-kissed gold.
A leap for the fruit, just out of reach,
I balanced like a goof, like a clumsy peach.

Squeezing through branches, I felt a tug,
Oops! Down came a fruit, like a big red bug.
I laughed with the gusts, the trees wagged their leaves,
As I made silly vows, like, 'No pie for thieves!'

Nearby, a crow cawed, with a cheeky delight,
Mocking my antics, what a comical sight!
I waved my arms wide, said, "You can't have my fun!"
While dodging more fruits that could weigh a ton.

Back in the wagon, I bruised my last prize,
But with laughter and joy, I still claimed the skies.
For every sweet moment, my heart felt so bright,
In that orchard adventure, I'd dance through the night.

Beneath the Harvest Moon

Beneath a round moon, the night feels alive,
We gather together, the brave and the sly.
With laughter, we plotted, as the shadows grew long,
To shake down the fruits, all while singing our song.

A bucket in hand and a cap on my head,
I climbed up a branch – should've stayed instead!
My foot slipped and flew, a comical scene,
Landing in soft grass, a king without a queen.

The full moon just chuckled, beaming down bright,
As I swatted at bugs in my fruit-nymph fight.
We giggled and squealed, like children at play,
While munching on treasures that glowed like the day.

And as we departed, our laughter took flight,
With hopes we'd return, on another bright night.
Behind us we left not just fruit on the ground,
But a harvest of giggles, that sweet joy we found.

An Orchard of Memories

In an orchard of laughter, I gather my friends,
With baskets and chuckles, our joy never ends.
We dodge pesky bees, while chasing each dream,
And fall into puddles that bubble and gleam.

I grabbed at a branch, but it yanked me right back,
And down fell a snack, what a glorious whack!
With juice on my chin and a grin painted wide,
The fruit-stained memories are my favorite tide.

Under branches that sway, we danced with delight,
Stumbling and giggling, it felt just right.
"Count one, two, three!" we would shout in the air,
As the squirrels joined in, declaiming their flair.

So here's to the moments, the laughter, the fun,
Underneath a sky where we all shine like one.
In this orchard of memories, joy is the theme,
We'll weave through this life, like a wild, silly dream.

Glimmers of Red

With glimmers of red, the day feels so bold,
We march through the rows, the young and the old.
With baskets held high, we dodge and we weave,
As fruit tumbles down, what a sight to believe!

My friend tried to climb, with a laugh and a cheer,
But ended up swinging like a wild chandelier!
We rolled on the turf, our laughter rang loud,
As the trees bore witness, we made them so proud.

Each pluck was a chance for a silly encore,
A dance in the dirt, who could ask for more?
The sun laughed with us, painting joy on our cheeks,
While squirrels ached for handouts, with their little shrieks.

As twilight approached, painted soft reds and greens,
We packed up our treasures like magical dreams.
With hearts so content, we shared one last cheer,
In glimmers of red, our happiness clear!

A Symphony of Colors and Cravings

In orchards bright, we frolic and roam,
With baskets in hand, we're far from home.
Chasing the fruit that dangles with glee,
Hoping one day, it'll come home for tea.

With every pluck, a giggle erupts,
As squirrels scamper, all cheeks and chumps.
A pie in the sky and a cake in the air,
Who knew that harvest could spark so much flair!

Ripe rounds of rubies, we can't help but munch,
But watch for the core—it gives quite a crunch!
With sticky fingers and faces turned red,
The sweetest debauchery, so much to be fed!

When ciders are bubbling, and laughter is bold,
Each bite brings a story, each laugh turns to gold.
So gather your friends, let's raise up a cheer,
For fruity adventures, the best time of year!

Dreams Cradled in Nature's Embrace

In the sunny fields, we dash with delight,
Chasing bright fortunes, oh, what a sight!
With baskets in hand, we gather the best,
Pretending we're pros on a fruity quest.

With splashes of laughter, we tumble and roll,
Finding the juiciest prize is our goal.
Oh what a bounty, we shout and we cheer,
For nature's whimsy fills us with cheer!

Under the shadows, we stumble and play,
Tripping on roots, come what may!
A dream of a future, sweet pies that will rise,
With hopes of dessert dancing in our eyes.

We carve our desires into seeds of our fate,
Each nibble, a secret; oh, isn't it great?
So let's raise a toast to these moments so true,
For nature's embrace always feels brand new!

Cherry Lucks and Golden Hopes

Cherries hang bright on the branches so high,
With ladders and dreams, we reach for the sky.
Squeezing through bushes, oh, what a sight,
Eyes wide with wonder, hearts feeling light.

Gold glimmers bright, like the sun on my skin,
As sticky sweet nectar gets caught in the din.
With laughter that ripples, we claw for a bite,
Fighting for fruit, like it's a wild fight!

And if we get lucky, with luck on our side,
We may just unearth some treasures to bide.
Competing for flavors, it's quite the good game,
In this fruity kingdom, all glory and fame!

So swing by the fruit trees, join in the thrill,
With bowls full of gems, we gobble our fill.
Here's to the fun that our harvests will bring,
To laughter and joy in the sweet, juicy spring!

The Boughs Brimming with Promise

Boughs bend and sway with the weight of delight,
In this orchard circus, everything's right.
With a wink and a grin, we jump with a cheer,
For bountiful harvest, it's that time of year!

Swaying like dancers, the branches twist low,
Tempting us closer, come see what they show.
With visions of picnics and parties so grand,
We chase those sweet dreams, each pluck by our hand.

With baskets a-bulging and laughter anew,
The sun casts a glow, everything's bright hue.
Sipping on nectar, we twirl and we spin,
In this lively patch, let the fun begin!

So let's not forget as we gather our prize,
To leave room for joy, let our spirits rise!
Here's to the journey, the mirth that we share,
For the boughs brimming promise, it's a love affair!

In the Shade of Fruity Fantasies

In the orchard where the giggles grow,
The branches dance with fruits in tow.
We grab them quick, like thieves at night,
Who knew a pear could cause a fright?

The sun is bright, our hats askew,
With sticky hands and cheeks askew.
We make a splash, we shout with glee,
Next year's harvest planned — oh me, oh my!

Each bite a burst, a zany surprise,
As juice drips down and laughter flies.
We toss the cores, oh, what a sight!
Who knew fruit fights could feel so right?

Beneath the leafy overhead dome,
We scheme and dream of finding home.
A quirky thought — my fruit-filled day,
Can life be sweeter? Pudding, hooray!

Counting Stars Among the Trees

Beneath a sky of twinkling lights,
We gather fruits, to our delight.
With every toss and silly cheer,
We hope for magic in this sphere.

The stars above, they wink and wave,
As we all dare the trees to cave.
In every laugh, a secret shared,
We write our tales, both bold and weird.

With a splash of juice and silly faces,
We judge the trees and their tight spaces.
Who knew that picking fruits could lead
To dreams of pies — so joyous indeed!

So let the night bring dances bright,
As shadows creep and stars ignite.
In fruity fun, the dreams unfurl,
The laughter echoes, life's the whirl.

The Sweet Surrender of Autumn

As autumn paints with colors bold,
We venture in, both brave and rolled.
With barrels full and plans to whirl,
A funny twist — all fruit will swirl!

The crunch beneath our happy feet,
Is music sweet, our futures greet.
With every fruit that bounces high,
We plot and scheme, oh my, oh my!

In cider dreams, we take our stand,
With mugs and pies all close at hand.
A mischief made, a pear that flew,
Who knew that autumn had a skew?

The season's laugh, it fills the air,
As we stomp grapes, oh, we don't care.
With chuckles loud, we'll sing our tune,
In this sweet chaos, we find our boon.

Orchard of the Heart's Desires

In every nook, a fruit awaits,
With dreams wrapped up in golden crates.
We run amok, with giggles bright,
Who knew that cherries could bring such fright?

The trees confide their fruity ploys,
As fallen apples tease the boys.
With playful shouts, we race our fate,
In juicy messes, we congregate.

Our hearts are light, our minds a whirl,
With sticky hugs, the memories twirl.
A swinging basket, a daring throw,
This orchard, our stage, steals the show!

So let us dance with fruits so ripe,
In laughter's grasp, we find our type.
With every bite, our spirits soar,
In this fruity realm, who could ask for more?

A Symphony of Red

In the orchard, we gather 'round,
With baskets big and giggles abound.
The fruits up high tease our reach,
As we plot our next daring speech.

A ladders' dance, a wobbly sway,
I shout 'Catch me!' on this fine day.
The branches sway, they join the fun,
As we swing like monkeys, just on the run.

Juice drips down, bright and wild,
We're all like kids, sweet and styled.
With sticky fingers and laughter loud,
We wear our treasures like a proud crowd.

The recipe calls for a pinch of glee,
A sprinkle of chaos, a dash of spree.
As pie on our faces makes us all grin,
Who needs a reason? Let the fun begin!

Resonance of the Orchard

Clustered fruits in emerald glade,
We whirl around like a merry parade.
With a friendly tug and a gentle pull,
The branches bang, our hearts are full.

Sneaky squirrels eye our sweet loot,
While we dance with our harvest in pursuit.
We toss them high, with laughter so wide,
As if they're footballs, oh what a ride!

A sticky fight breaks the calming breeze,
With splashes of color among the trees.
A chipmunk cheers, or is it a friend?
All's well here, our joy won't end.

As dusk filters in, we sip our cider,
With jokes that soar, our spirits get lighter.
The evening glows, a whimsical show,
In this land where gloopy treasures flow.

Dawn in the Grove

The sun peeks through, a golden grin,
In the grove where mischief begins.
Our footsteps crunch on the leafy earth,
Sharing our dreams, and laughs of mirth.

The sweetest fruits hang, a cheeky display,
"Who can reach them?" we giggle and play.
Jump and stretch, our bounds we test,
While butterflies join this wild fest.

A soft breeze teases our hair in a swirl,
As we plot hilarious notions and twirls.
Oh, the ideas that float like confetti,
In this haven, where nature's so ready!

With baskets brimming, we dance like the breeze,
Happiness gleams in laughter with ease.
As the dawn spills gold, our dreams ignite,
In this grove, everything feels just right.

Sweet Serendipity

Amidst the trees, a right little game,
We gather the bounty, but who's to blame?
For taking a bite before it's quite fair,
"Just checking for sweetness!" fills the air.

A friendly bet of who'll bring the most,
As we tumble and giggle, our laughter's the toast.
The bees seem to buzz in a rhythm or tune,
As we sway in the glow of the afternoon.

With a clang and a bang, our laughter ignites,
As we play tug-of-war, oh what a sight!
Fragrant delights in a sticky embrace,
With cheerful mishaps, we find our place.

Then into pies our treasures go,
With sprinkles of magic in every flow.
We savor the sweetness, our hearts invite,
In this moment of joy, everything's bright!

Ripe with Possibility

In the tree they dangle, red and bright,
I reach for one, with all my might.
But it slips right through, what a sight!
Landing on my head, quite the fright!

The squirrels are laughing, oh what fun,
Chasing after me, just on the run.
I grab a basket, but I'm outdone,
Now I'm the punchline, under the sun!

The birds are singing, teasing me too,
As I stumble about, in this fruit-strewn zoo.
I dream of cider, a hearty brew,
Yet all I have is this sticky goo!

With every tug on a branch, I shall see,
These juicy treasures, laughing at me.
How many apples can one heart decree?
Filled with giggles, that's the key!

Nature's Pantry of Desire.

A basket full of wishes spills in my hand,
I think I'll share, but don't understand.
Why does the neighbor's dog make a stand?
Barking at me, like he's in command!

I climb a ladder, oh, what a dance,
The apples above, they seem to prance.
I stretch and I reach, oh, what a chance,
But down I go, without a glance!

The laughter echoes, it tickles my toes,
As my friend says, "At this rate, you'll doze!"
But my heart is light, despite all my woes,
For who knew fruit could come with such shows?

A plump one winks, it jests with a grin,
I swear it's plotting, some devilish kin.
To roll off the branch, where does it begin?
To find the right wish, oh let's just spin!

Harvest Dreams

A harvest awaits with a giggling flair,
I dream of pie but find only air.
My friends all tease, 'You best beware!'
Underneath the tree, I've lost my hair!

Each apple I spot seems to give me a wink,
While I'm standing here, with no time to think.
The bees are buzzing in a wild sync,
I dodge and weave, like a carnival link!

One misstep over and down I go,
Rolling like fruit, on this merry show.
The raccoons are giggling, stealing the glow,
As I ponder again, where did my safe place go?

A harvest of laughter, that's what I gain,
With every bump and every strain.
In this orchard of joy, I fully remain,
Wishing for apples, but finding the rain!

Orchard Whispers

In the orchard's heart, secrets abound,
Apples lean close, whispering sound.
They spill tales of dreams from the ground,
Where wishes are wild, and laughter is found.

A windy breeze carries giggles through leaves,
While I try to pluck, and the branch heaves.
It chuckles at me, as the sun weaves,
Making mischief, like a jester, it believes!

One slips and rolls, a jolly old tease,
I chase it down, through the grass and trees.
But nature giggles, as I end on my knees,
With a mouth full of dirt and the wildest of cheese!

Yet nothing can stop me, not even a fall,
I gather these moments, each giggly sprawl.
For in this wild world, I have it all,
A heart full of laughter, I heed the call!

www.ingramcontent.com/pod-product-compliance
Lightning Source LLC
Chambersburg PA
CBHW060143230426
43661CB00003B/544